GW01236997

Windows on the
Growing up in Differe

Selected by Chris Powling

For Anne Marley and librarians everywhere

Contents

Section 1
Ahmed's Secret Florence Parry Heide   2
From *The Day Of Ahmed's Secret*

My Crummy Mummy Anne Fine   6
From *Crummy Mummy and Me*

Section 2
Ghost Trouble Ruskin Bond   10
From *Ghost Trouble*

A Chilly Night in Africa Tony Fairman   13
From *Bury My Bones But Keep My Words*

From Granny's Rooftop Adèle Geras   16
From *My Grandmother's Stories*

Section 3
Adopting Mowgli Rudyard Kipling   22
From *The Jungle Book*

Night Attack Beverly Naidoo   28
From *No Turning Back*

In the extracts which follow you'll jet around the world faster than any aeroplane can carry you. Each visit will be pretty short … but if you want to stay a little longer, no problem. Simply go to your local library and borrow the book from which the extract comes. Libraries are the cheapest and handiest of all travel-shops!

Let's begin in a faraway city …

Longman

Edinburgh Gate
Harlow, Essex

ST. JOSEPH'S CATHOLIC PRIMARY SCHOOL
MOUNTAIN VIEW, COCKERMOUTH
CUMBRIA CA13 0DG
Telephone/Fax: (01900) 325932

Ahmed's Secret

The first place I go is the home of the old woman. She has been waiting for me. "Ahmed! Ahmed!" she calls. "Are you bringing me the fuel for my stove?"

The old woman is leaning out of her window. I look up and smile. I am proud that I can carry these big heavy bottles all the way up the steps to the floor where she lives. I am proud that I can do this work to help my family.

I make more stops, and now I am hungry again. I look for the bright red and yellow cart where I can buy my lunch, and I find it in its usual place near the old building. I buy my beans and rice, and sit in the shade of the old wall. My father has told me the wall is a thousand years old, and even our great-great-grandfathers were not yet born when it was built. There are many old buildings, many old walls like the one I lean against, in this city.

I close my eyes and have my quiet time, the time my father says I must have each day. "If there are no quiet spaces in your head, it fills with noise," he has told me.

He has shown me how to find my way in the city, and he has taken me to each place where I now have to bring the heavy bottles. In those days before I was strong enough to do this work alone, I would sit in the cart and watch my father lift and carry the bottles. One day I told him that now I could do it by myself. He watched me try to take a heavy bottle from the cart. I could not do it, and I was ashamed.

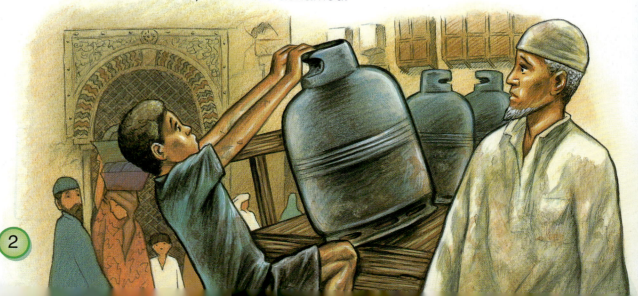

"Hurry to grow strong, Ahmed," my father said on that day. For the first time I saw that his face had a tired look, like the faces of the old men in the city. "Hurry to grow strong," he said again. "But do not hurry to grow old."

Now as I lean against the old building, I think of the sea of sand that lies along our city. I have seen it, stretching as far as the wind. My father says the wind carries sand all through the city to remind us that the desert is there, is there beside us, and is part of us. He tells me that the great desert presses against our city on one side, and the great river pushes against it on the other. "We live between them," my father has said. "Between our two friends, the river and the desert."

All over the world, people know of our city, he tells me, and they speak of its name: Cairo. And they say the name of our great river: the Nile. "And the desert, what is that called?" I ask. My father shrugs and smiles. "The hot winds call our desert home." He himself has never crossed the desert. But in the city are the caravans of camels and their riders who have crossed it many times, the way the boats cross and re-cross the river.

I lean against the wall and I think of these things and of my secret, but I must finish my work before I go home. First I try to knock the sand from my sandals. The sand is a part of each day, like the noise, like the colours of the city, like the things my father has said. On the way to my next stop I see the boy who carries bread. From a window a girl lowers a basket to him on a rope, and he puts some bread in the basket. Like me, he has many stops to make each day, but he is not strong enough to do what I do. No one lowers a rope to me for my heavy loads! No rope could carry what I carry.

I hear the rose-water man before I see him. He clicks two cups together as he walks along the street so people will hear him and come to him for a drink. I give him my smile. He does not give me his, but our eyes meet and we know we are connected to the same day and to the city. I do not buy his rose-water, but seeing him has reminded me how hot and thirsty I am. I take a drink from the bottle of water I always carry in my cart.

There are more stops to make, and more times up and up narrow steps with my heavy load, and then I am back in my cart. *Karink, rink rink, karink, rink rink.* It is a long day. I think the moment will never come when I may share my secret, but of course I know that each day ends and that every moment has its time to be.

So what is Ahmed's secret? For the full story, read *The Day of Ahmed's Secret* by Florence Parry Heide. On the very last page we find out that Ahmed can write his own name – a real achievement for a boy who has to work all day instead of going to school.

Our next trip brings us much closer to home …

My Crummy Mummy

I don't think my mum's fit to be a parent, really I don't. Every morning it's the same, every single morning. I'm standing by the front door with my coat on, ready to go. School starts at nine and it's already eight-forty or even later, and she's not ready. She's not even nearly ready. Sometimes she isn't even dressed.

"Come *on*," I shout up the stairs. "We have to leave now."

"Hang on a minute!"

"What are you *doing* up there?"

Her voice comes, all muffled, through the bedroom door: "Nothing."

"You *must* be doing something," I yell.

"I'm *not*."

"Come down, then. We're *waiting*."

"Can't find my shoes."

I lean against the front door, sighing. With as much patience as I can muster, I call upstairs: "Where did you take them off?"

"I *thought* I took them off in the bathroom …"

"Look there, then."

"I *have*."

"If you would only put your shoes away neatly at night, we wouldn't have to go through this every single morning!"

By now, of course, my baby sister's fretting. She's strapped inside her pushchair and since I put her coat and bonnet on at least ten minutes ago, and she's still indoors, her head and ears are getting hot and scratchy. She's boiling up into one of her little rages. Already she's trying to tug her bonnet off.

"Will you come *on*?" I shout upstairs. (I'm really getting mad now.)

"I'm coming. I'm coming!"

"Well, hurry *up*!"

At last, she comes downstairs. And even then she's never dressed right. You'd think, honestly you would, that we didn't have any windows upstairs, the way she chooses what to wear. She certainly can't bother to look through them at the weather. She'll sail down in midwinter, when it's snowing, in a thin cotton frock with short puffy sleeves, and no woolly.

I have to be firm. "You can't come out like that."

"Why not?"

"You just can't," I tell her. "You'll catch your death. It's snowing out there. It's *far* too cold for bare arms. You'll freeze."

"I'll put a coat on."

But I just stare at her until she goes back upstairs for a sweater. And even then she'll choose something quite unsuitable. She never dresses in the right sort of thing. She'd wear her glittery legwarmers to a funeral if I let her (or if we ever went to funerals). She'd sit on a beach in her thick purple poncho. If she were called in to see the headmaster, she'd rather wear those baggy flowery shorts she found abandoned on a park bench last Easter than anything sensible. She'd look fantastic – she always does – but not at all like a mother. You have to watch her. You can't let up.

At least she admits it. "I'm a terrible embarrassment to you, Minna," she confesses, buckling on two of her best studded belts. "I'm a Crummy Mummy."

Then I feel mean for being so stern. "You're not a Crummy Mummy," I tell her. "You do your best. And I suppose it doesn't *really* matter what you look like …"

"You're right," she says, cheering up at once. And then, if you let her, she'd get worse. At least, that's what my gran says, and she should know because she's like my mother.

I like my gran. She lives right on the other side of the estate, but she comes over almost every tea-time. She picks Miranda out of the cot, and coos to her, and then she sits with Miranda on her knee on the only bit of the sofa that isn't leaking stuffing. Mostly, she tells Mum off. She says now Mum's a mother of two, it's time she grew up and pulled herself together. She tells Mum she should throw all her safety-pin earrings and lavender fishnet tights into the dustbin, and go out and buy herself a nice, decent frock from Marks and Spencer. She says Mum ought to take those horrible Punk Skunks records off the stereo before they ruin Miranda, and put on something nice and easy to listen to, like Perry Como's Christmas Selection.

And then, if Mum hasn't flounced off in a huff, Gran purses her lips together as if she's been sucking lemons and, clutching Miranda so tightly her dummy pops out of her mouth and her face goes purple, she whispers to Mum that she's clearly still very much under the influence of that dreadful, _dreadful –_

Here, she looks around shiftily, and drops her voice even lower: "I don't even want to say his _name_ in front of innocent children, but you know exactly who I mean."

I know exactly who she means, too. She means Crusher Maggot, that's who she means. Crusher Maggot is Mum's boyfriend. It was me who first called him Crusher Maggot because that's what he looks like, and when he first started coming round here I didn't like him. Now I like him a lot, but it's too late. The nickname's stuck. He doesn't mind, though. And now even Mum calls him Crusher Maggot.

There's more about Crusher Maggot, Miranda, Gran and Minna's Crummy Mummy in Anne Fine's _Crummy Mummy and Me_. It's a reminder that families just like ours may not be **exactly** like ours!

Now let's meet a ghost …

Ghost Trouble

It was Grandfather who finally decided that we would have to move to another house. And it was all because of a Pret, a mischievous north-Indian ghost, who had been making life difficult for everyone.

Prets usually live in peepal trees, and that's where our little ghost first had his home – in the branches of a massive old peepal tree which had grown through the compound wall and spread into our garden. Part of the tree was on our side of the wall, part on the other side, shading the main road. It gave the ghost a good view of the whole area.

For many years the Pret had lived there quite happily, without bothering anyone in our house. It did not bother me, either, and I spent a lot of time in the peepal tree. Sometimes I went there to escape the adults at home, sometimes to watch the road and the people who passed by. The peepal tree was cool on a hot day, and the heart-shaped leaves were always revolving in the breeze. This constant movement of the leaves also helped to disguise the movements of the Pret, so that I never really knew exactly where he was sitting. But he paid no attention to me. The traffic on the road kept him fully occupied.

Sometimes, when a tonga was passing, he would jump down and frighten the pony, and as a result the little pony-cart would go rushing off in the wrong direction. Sometimes he would get into the engine of a car or a bus, which would have a breakdown soon afterwards. And he liked to knock the sun-helmets off the heads of sahibs or officials, who would wonder how a strong breeze had sprung up so suddenly, only to die down just as quickly. Although this special kind of ghost could make himself felt, and sometimes heard, he was invisible to the human eye.

I was not invisible to the human eye, and often got the blame for some of the Pret's pranks. If bicycle-riders were struck by mango seeds or apricot stones, they would look up, see a small boy in the branches of the tree, and threaten me with terrible consequences. Drivers who went off after parking their cars in the shade would sometimes come back to find their tyres flat. My protests of innocence did not carry much weight. But when I mentioned the Pret in the tree, they would look uneasy, either because they thought I must be mad, or because they were afraid of ghosts, especially Prets. They would find other things to do and hurry away …

Eventually, in Ruskin Bond's story *Ghost Trouble*, the family does move away. You'd better get hold of the book, though, if you think this cures the problem.

Our next stop is Botswana …

A Chilly Night in Africa

I expect you think it's always hot in Africa, don't you …?… Well, in some parts, way down in the south, they have winter and it gets cold at night. The leaves fall off the trees, everything stops growing and there are no insects. You have to wrap up well because sometimes there's a frost at night.

It's chilly tonight. Not cold enough for frost yet, but there's a fire out in the courtyard. There's no moon, but the stars are up there in the black sky – millions of tiny, silent pinholes flung all over the black hood of night.

And here comes Grandma shuffling outside into the courtyard. She sits with her feet towards the fire and pulls a blanket round her shoulders to keep her back warm. She picks up a long branch and pushes one end of it into the fire. A flame flares out and sparks shoot up to join the stars overhead.

In the light of the flame you can see the round house with its overhanging thatch and the low wall that surrounds the clean-swept courtyard. The wall and the house are painted with patterns of squares and circles, and over the door you can read BLESS THIS HOUSE.

Inside the house there are sounds of people working. There's always work to be done and mother does most of it. Her children, Tebogo and his little sister, Tshipidi, help as much as they can. But inside the house it's always Mother who cooks, washes and cleans. And outside the house it's always Mother who does most of the digging, weeding and harvesting of the crops.

When Mother and the children have finished their jobs inside the house, they come out carrying blankets, one for the children and one for Mother. They sit down side by side with their feet towards the fire next to Grandma, and wrap the blankets right round themselves and in a peak over their heads. From behind they look like small tents. It's chilly tonight, nippy on the nose and ears.

Tebogo is twelve years old and is proud of the English he's learnt at school. He likes to teach his little sister, Tshipidi, who's only seven. "Good morning. How are you?" he says.

"Goomorring. Ow ow you?" Tshipidi repeats and Tebogo tries to correct her. Sometimes she says "Goomorring" in the evening, but Tebogo doesn't

BLESS THIS HOUSE

14

correct her because his English lessons are always in the morning, so he hasn't learnt to say "Good afternoon" or "Good evening".

"Grandma," says Tebogo, "I can see a long story stick in the fire. Are you going to tell us a long story tonight?"

"No," says Grandma, "you know all my stories. Your mother can tell you a different story tonight."

Overhead, the pinhole stars are twinkling, and beyond the courtyard wall the shapes of flat-topped thorn trees flicker in the firelight, white, like trees in a negative.

Mother says, "All right then, I'll tell about the man with a tree on his head. But it won't be a long story. It's getting cold and I'm tired. So we'll burn the branch quickly and make the story short."

And it's a very strange tale that mother tells. To hear it, find Tony Fairman's book *Bury My Bones But Keep My Words*, which brings together stories from all over Africa. Of course, storytelling parents and grandparents can be found everywhere in the world.

In Jerusalem, for instance …

15

From Granny's Rooftop

Outside the front door of my grandmother's flat there was a flight of stairs leading to the roof: a wide, flat area bordered by a stone parapet where all the families in the building used to hang their washing. If you went up on laundry day, the whole roof was aflutter with damp sheets and tablecloths, flapping shirts and blouses, scarves like flags waving, flocks of white handkerchiefs like doves, and here and there, strange and wonderful garments which made my cousins and me laugh behind my grandmother's back: Mrs Sirkis's huge lace-edged bloomers, and the long, skinny, striped socks belonging to the dentist who lived on the first floor. The clothes on the washing line smelled strongly of pale yellow soap, and were held on the line by wooden clothespegs that had been bleached pale grey by the sun. My grandmother used to bring the wet clothes up to the roof in a big tin tub. This tub had a handle on each side, and once the clothes were pegged out, it was light enough for me to hold on to one of the handles and help my grandmother carry it downstairs again.

The roof seemed very high up to me. There were days when it frightened me to look over the parapet and down, down, down into the street. Far below us, I could see the door to Genzel's shop, and although the things that people were buying were in their baskets as they came out, my grandmother knew exactly what everyone had gone to the shop for.

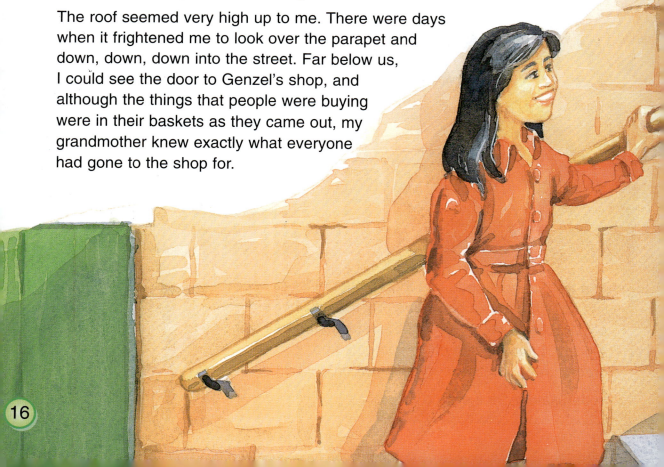

"There's Mrs Rakov buying herrings," she'd say. "She is making chopped herring tonight. Look, there's Mr Lapidas, he's bought some bagels and cream cheese … that's what he likes for his lunch, bagels and cheese … Mrs Blumberg needs onions … there were none in her kitchen yesterday … this I saw with my own eyes …" and so on.

I liked going to Genzel's shop. It was so near the flat that sometimes my grandmother would put money in my hand and send me down there for something: a few grams of cheese or a packet of tea. I followed the stairs, round and round and round from the third floor to the street, quite by myself, and then I carefully crossed over the little side road and went into the dark treasure-cave of Genzel's shop. I wasn't frightened because I knew that my grandmother was watching me from the balcony, and I always waved at her from the corner. Genzel's shelves were filled with tins and boxes, and the small room smelled of soap and salt and cheese and wax, the silver herrings bobbing in the big, brown barrel, the shiny black olives floating in inky water, and the round yellow cheeses on the counter. Sacks of flour stood open by the entrance, and there were sweets in glass jars near the drawer where Mrs Genzel kept her money. Strings of onions hung from the ceiling, and tall people went into the shop with their heads bent. Genzel was thin and wore a dusty black jacket. Mrs Genzel was fat and if you didn't watch out, she'd pinch your cheek between her thumb and forefinger, muttering endearments, or even give you a fishy-smelling kiss. I used to ask for whatever I wanted and Genzel would get it for me, wrap it in newspaper and put it in my basket, and take my money and give me change. Mrs Genzel would give me a wonderful sweet like a marble that tasted of aniseed and changed colour as I sucked it.

My cousin Danny and I had a special game that we used to play on the roof. We'd collected lots of broken clothespegs and hidden the tiny pieces of wood under a bucket. We used to wait until a man wearing a hat went past, far below us in the street, and then we'd throw a piece of peg over the parapet and lean over to see whether it had landed in the man's hat, or at least near enough to make him look up. If anyone *did* look up, we used to crouch down where we couldn't be seen and laugh and laugh.

One day in spring, as I was looking over the edge, waiting for my grandmother to finish hanging out the washing, I saw something astonishing.

"Come quickly and look," I said to my grandmother. There's a man walking past with an animal curled round his head … it must be asleep."
My grandmother looked. "Silly girl! Haven't you seen a streimel before?"
"What's a streimel?"
"A hat with fur all round the crown."
"Oh … well, maybe I have seen one … but it looks different from up here. Not like a fur hat at all. Just like a cat wrapped round the man's head. Why is he wearing a fur hat on such a warm day?"

"Because it's a kind of uniform. It shows that that man is very religious. He spends most of his days studying the scriptures. His mind, you see, is on higher things than hats, or whether he's feeling too warm. He may even," said my grandmother, "be a rabbi. You know what a rabbi is, don't you?"
"Oh, yes," I said. "He takes services in the synagogue."
"And that's not all he does," said my grandmother. "Rabbis have to be especially clever men, not only because they are dealing with God's work all day long, but also because they have to give advice, settle arguments, help everyone to live together peacefully … it's a difficult job, I can tell you."

In this case, the writer is Adèle Geras who lives in Manchester nowadays but grew up in Israel. Her book, *My Grandmother's Stories*, is full of such childhood memories.

Lucky Adèle! Some youngsters start life in rather more risky circumstances …

Adopting Mowgli

The bushes rustled a little in the thicket, and Father Wolf dropped with his haunches under him, ready for his leap. Then, if you had been watching, you would have seen the most wonderful thing in the world – the wolf checked in mid-spring. He made his bound before he saw what it was he was jumping at, and then he tried to stop himself. The result was that he shot up straight into the air for four or five feet, landing almost where he left the ground.

"Man!" he snapped. "A man's cub. Look!" Directly in front of him, holding on by a low branch, stood a naked brown baby who would just walk – as soft and as dimpled a little atom as ever came to a wolf's cave at night. He looked up into Father Wolf's face, and laughed.

"Is that a man's cub?" said Mother Wolf. "I have never seen one. Bring it here."

A wolf accustomed to moving his own cubs can, if necessary, mouth an egg without breaking it, and though Father Wolf's jaws closed right on the child's back not a tooth even scratched the skin, as he laid it down among the cubs.

"How little! How naked, and – how bold!" said Mother Wolf softly. The baby was pushing his way between the cubs to get close to the warm hide. "Ahai! He is taking his meal with the others. And so this is a man's cub. Now, was there ever a wolf that could boast of a man's cub among her children?"

"I have heard now and again of such a thing, but never in our Pack or in my time," said Father Wolf. "He is altogether without hair, and I could kill him with a touch of my foot. But see, he looks up and is not afraid."

The moonlight was blocked out of the mouth of the cave, for Shere Khan's great square head and shoulders were thrust into the entrance. Tabaqui, behind him, was squeaking: "My lord, my lord, it went in here!"

"Shere Khan does us great honour," said Father Wolf, but his eyes were very angry. "What does Shere Khan need?"

"My quarry. A man's cub went this way," said Shere Khan. "Its parents have run off. Give it to me."

Shere Khan had jumped at a woodcutter's campfire, as Father Wolf had said, and was furious from the pain of his burned feet. But Father Wolf knew that the mouth of the cave was too narrow for a tiger to come in by. Even where he was, Shere Khan's shoulders and forepaws were cramped for want of room, as a man's would be if he tried to fight in a barrel.

"The Wolves are a free people," said Father Wolf. "They take orders from the Head of the Pack, and not from any striped cattle-killer. The man's cub is ours – to kill if we choose."

"Ye choose and ye do not choose! What talk is this of choosing? By the bull that I killed, am I to stand nosing into your dog's den for my fair dues? It is I, Shere Khan, who speak!"

The tiger's roar filled the cave with thunder. Mother Wolf shook herself clear of the cubs and sprang forward, her eyes, like two green moons in the darkness, facing the blazing eyes of Shere Khan. "And it is I, Raksha (The Demon), who answer. The man's cub is mine, Lungri – mine to me! He shall not be killed. He shall live to run with the Pack and to hunt with the Pack; and in the end, look you, hunter of little naked cubs – frog-eater – fish-killer – he shall hunt *thee*! Now get hence, or by the Sambhur that I killed (I eat no starved cattle), back thou goest to thy mother, burned beast of the Jungle, lamer than ever thou camest into the world! Go!"

Father Wolf looked on amazed. He had almost forgotten the days when he won Mother Wolf in fair fight from five other wolves, when she ran in the Pack and was not called The Demon for compliment's sake. Shere Khan might have faced Father Wolf, but he could not stand up against Mother Wolf, for he knew that where he was she had all the advantage of the ground, and would fight to the death. So he backed out of the cave-mouth growling, and when he was clear he shouted: "Each dog barks in his own yard! We will see what the Pack will say to this fostering of man-cubs. The cub is mine, and to my teeth he will come in the end, O bush-tailed thieves!"

Mother Wolf threw herself down panting among the cubs, and Father Wolf said to her gravely: "Shere Khan speaks this much truth. The cub must be shown to the Pack. Wilt thou still keep him, Mother?"

"Keep him!" she gasped. "He came naked, by night, alone and very hungry; yet he was not afraid! Look, he has pushed one of my babes to one side already. And that lame butcher would have killed him and would have run off to the Waingunga while the villagers here hunted through all our lairs in revenge! Keep him? Assuredly I will keep him. Lie still, little frog. O thou Mowgli – for Mowgli the Frog I will call thee – the time will come when thou wilt hunt Shere Khan as he has hunted thee."

Rudyard Kipling's *The Jungle Book* is the most famous of all stories about children being brought up by wild animals. He was drawing on the jungle he remembered from his own boyhood in India, but it's fair to say that what comes out on the page is much more like the jungle of his, and our, imagination.

Mind you, there are different kinds of jungle …

Night Attack

Sipho must have fallen asleep. Because the next thing he knew was that he was waking up in the terror that usually came from a nightmare. The kind of nightmare in which his stepfather turned into a monster with ten heads and ten pairs of arms and legs. In this terror now, however, there were screams and shouts and the sharp pain of a boot being kicked into his ribs. Thick hands were grabbing him. He tried to struggle but he was caught in a vice, squeezing his wrists and twisting his arms behind his back. In the beam of a light flashing wildly, he saw the writhing bodies of the other boys and the grinning faces of their captors. They were being hauled across the pozzie out into the road and then thrown into the back of a gumba-gumba, a dreaded police van. Lucas, the last to be slung in, fell like a sack of potatoes and the van doors were banged shut.

For a minute no one said anything. Sipho was shaking. Jabu was holding his side and whimpering. Everyone was in shock. Then the silence broke in the dark. "What do they want with us?"
"Who are these people?"
"Police! Only police drive gumba-gumbas."
"But they don't have uniforms."
"They take off their uniform when they want to do something bad so you can't say for sure it's them."
"They stole my knife! If I had my knife I would kill them!"

Sipho clutched himself more tightly, his eyes adjusting slowly to the darkness. Lucas was painfully lifting himself up. He spoke quietly. "We don't know how many of these are police. They can get into trouble for this kind of thing now."

Perhaps only one or two were actual policemen, continued Lucas. The others could be their friends … the kind of white people who didn't want any change in the country … who wanted to keep black people down forever and who didn't want them to vote in the elections for the new government.

Suddenly from outside the van there was a burst of laughter. A few seconds later the van doors were wrenched open. Sipho made out a hand being thrust in, then the sound of squirting. Even before the hand was pulled back and the door slammed shut, something was in their eyes, their nostrils, their mouths. There was no air left to breathe, only something horribly foul stifling them. It smelt like the spray for killing insects. Coughing and trying to cover his mouth at the same time, Sipho felt he was going to be sick.

Now the gumba-gumba was moving, its engine revving and rumbling. Where were they being taken? It felt like they were travelling at speed, only occasionally slowing down. Together they clustered at the far end of the van, holding on to each other, holding their stomachs tightly or trying to bury their faces and stinging eyes in their arms.

Suddenly the van gave an enormous shudder and Sipho found himself flung forward as it came to a bumping halt. He was the first to be grabbed as the door swung open. "OK, vuilgoed! Rubbish like you can get a nice wash here!" Ahead of him, glinting through the darkness, Sipho saw water. He screamed as he was picked up. He tried to struggle once again but it was no use. The hands and arms were too powerful for him as they threw him out into the lake.

Hitting, then breaking through the ice-cold water, his body shot out arms and legs in all directions. He couldn't swim. The more he fought with the water to get back up, the more he felt it pulling him down. He was spluttering. The water was in his nose, in his mouth … He couldn't breathe. He was sinking, his body pierced by a thousand freezing shocks.

Then a hand grasped his arm and he felt himself being slowly tugged until his foot touched something. Something solid which wasn't sinking beneath him. He brought his other foot down. He was standing! Stretching, he got his head enough above the water to gasp and gulp at the air. The hand led him on a few more paces then let go. A figure dived away from him. He was too confused to know who it was. Cries mingled with wild splashing sounds. On the bank ahead, he could just make out two large figures throwing a struggling shape out into the lake. Lucas? Laughter floated over to him. The gumba-gumba was revving up again. Within seconds the men had all climbed inside and disappeared into the night.

Underneath his feet, Sipho felt things that were sharp. Painfully edging step by step, he forced himself forward through the water. His clothes, dripping and sticking to his body, felt unusually heavy. Shivering uncontrollably, he waded at last to the water's edge, pulled himself on to the bank and flung himself down on his back. Directly above, as if staring down at him from the ink-black sky, was the moon, pale and white. Like a face. Was it laughing too?

One by one the other malunde joined him, shaking, swearing, sobbing. Jabu was the last. His head bobbing, in and out of the water, going down here and coming up there, he guided those who were struggling towards the bank. Such a strong swimmer …

This is the jungle of Johannesburg in South Africa – a city jungle, full of street kids like Sipho, described in Beverley Naidoo's novel *No Turning Back.* For some children every day is a struggle to survive. Read this gritty narrative to learn more about Sipho's fate.